OVERCOMING YOUR

EVIL TWIN

Is Your Mind Playing Tricks on You?

PAT PILLA

DISCLAIMER

The sole purpose of this book is to educate and inspire. There is no guarantee made by the author or the publisher that anyone following the ideas, tips, suggestions, techniques or strategies will become successful. The author and publisher shall have neither liability nor responsibility to anyone with respect to any loss or damage caused, or alleged to be caused, directly or indirectly by the information contained in this book.

As a coach and mentor, I have been truly blessed and inspired by everyone that crossed my path and the ones I were able to love, encourage and guide to the next level in their life journey.

This book is dedicated to each one of you.

My coaching spans across the world and to be blessed to talk with you and ignite that fire and bring your passion into fruition, well, that is just an extra bonus.

We are all here to serve one another and when you use your unique gift that God empowered you with, all I can say to YOU is YOU make me proud and you have changed my life and inspired me as well.

May God's blessings be yours forever and ever. Thank you for being you and being in my life.

CONTENTS

PAT PILLA

FOREWORD

*O*vercoming *Your Evil Twin* is truly a masterpiece! I literally read it from cover to cover in a few hours. There is so much wisdom in these pages, I literally felt like a different man by the time I finished it.

Pat has a beautiful way of expressing what's in her heart through the written word. This book has the ability to change your outlook forever.

You learn through Pat's powerful stories and first-hand wisdom. I am truly honored to write the foreword to such a piece of art, and believe me I'm buying copies for my loved ones. *Overcoming your Evil Twin* is that good!

This book should be in all schools as a compass for understanding one's "Evil Twin," I wish I had read this book when I was younger, it would have saved me years of pain and turmoil.

If you're looking for a change in your life, this is the book, I promise you. Read it with an open mind because the insights you will gather from this book will be ground breaking and it will change your perspective on life.

AJ Mihrzad

Best-selling Author

Founder, OnlineSupercoach.com

PREFACE

Everyone has the same voice playing in their heads. It's just at different "volumes" and with different amounts of "influence."

—Manny Wolfe

I was inspired to write this book because of my so called mind chatter - AKA "evil twin" - used to wreak havoc on me. I didn't know who to believe. My tendencies to doubt and sabotage myself had my evil twin working overtime. I never believed in myself because I didn't love myself to the degree to say, "I am enough!"

Each chapter in this book is going to help you recognize when your evil twin shows up, and take the steps to tame this pesky little twit. You are going to rid yourself of self-inflicted pain and become the person you were meant to be.

PAT PILLA

It took me years to discover the simple truth that, *"Yes, I am worth something and God created me for greatness."* My turning point came when I was so overweight that I could barely breathe. I felt I was totally useless; not only to myself, but to others around me as well.

I searched for that "something better" that I knew was out there for me, but could not find it. After some self-reflection, I resolved to stop chasing things that were "outside of myself" and there began my journey. I prayed with intensity and as my faith grew steadily stronger, I understood that I had to change.

Here I was, always looking to outside sources when in reality, I already possessed all that I needed to succeed. It was all there. I just had to tap into it. And I did!

Growing up was a horror for me. Going to school as an overweight child was torture. I was picked on and ridiculed every single day. When I returned home from school, it wasn't any better. Without a safe haven, I continually turned to my comfort of the day – food – or more specifically, dessert. I was literally eating myself to death.

Society saw me as a fat slob who couldn't control herself, and didn't understand the agony of my pain. My whole life, I've overheard these cruel words, "What a shame ... she has such a pretty face. If she could just lose weight!" Everyone looked at me with disgust, or at least that is how my evil twin made me feel. No one ever explained to me that I was using food to mask my inner demons, to pacify the hurt and struggle.

My evil twin was filling my mind with a novel of lies, and I believed them. The more obese I became, the louder her voice grew. I could not bear the negativity and the hopelessness, and at what felt like the point of no return, I thought of ending it all. Hopelessness drove me deeper into my depression, so much so that I began to feel comfortable being depressed. Every negative word I repeated to myself fed into a churning cycle of self-loathing. I'll tell you a secret: for an entire summer, I never left the house. It's hard to believe this now, but I was so embarrassed by the way I looked that I would not go out without a coat to hide behind. Being a hermit was becoming my new life. I knew my life had hit rock bottom, and I didn't know how to get out of it. In my eyes, I was a wasted soul.

When you hit the bottom, you only have two choices. You can either pick yourself up -- or die. I decided to get back up. I began reading about other people who had transformations, about their hopes and how they succeeded. I prayed to God to find people who would help me. My affirmation was "If they can do it, so can I." I started loving the word "HOPE!" And God answered my prayers and positioned the right people on my path. I now had the courage and the power to fight and continue the journey towards my purpose.

No doubt, there were times when I wanted to give up. I found strength through God when I began to read my Bible more and more. God's Word said that I was created in His image, and that I was FEARFULLY and WONDERFULLY made. At that very moment, I realized that God does not make junk. Those words gave me the strength to go on; that statement became real to me and still brings tears to my eyes when I hear it. I did not know anyone could feel that way about me or love me so deeply. No one had ever said that I was wonderfully made, but if God said it, I believe it.

So I continued to tap into that power and I found the will to carry on and discover my true gifts. I knew there was a reason why I was created, and I could now change my situation, because I found love. I *finally* loved myself and found myself worthy of receiving my special gift; my gift that I am now sharing with you.

I don't want to see anyone struggle with who they are and what they were meant to be. We need to live with passion and a purpose, and that passion is your gift.

—Me!

You have to stop every now and then to reflect on the values that you hold so dear. Your values are the dreams and visions that fuel your heart, and what keeps you going through tough times. We all have a purpose and what we do reflects on each one of us. You are so important to this world, that without you, we would suffer. That is how precious you are.

You may be searching for your superpower, your unique gift that you were born to give to this world. It's a scary process - we can become so scared that we start doubting ourselves. In this book, I will tell you how you can tap into your uniqueness and find your superpower.

You don't have to go on being unfulfilled and not living your truth. The truth is that you have a gift. You are unique and no one – yes, no one - has what you have. I want to show you how you can unwrap your wonderful gift and share it with the world.

You will no longer feel like you are living a mediocre life, or feel dead inside. You will feel vibrant and more energized when you begin each day. You have a purpose (and so do I), and together we *can* and *will* make a change and a difference.

You must believe that the world needs you, and that you were created for a far greater purpose than you are living now. Your talent is yearning to emerge so don't deny yourself or others your unique superpower because you have lost faith. Don't lose hope in yourself like I did because of an evil twin lurking inside your mind.

Let's break out of playing it safe and keeping yourself comfortable, because being safe and secure is not going to make you shine. You need to forge ahead through the storms to reach that rainbow on the other side. The pot of gold at the end of that rainbow is your light shining in this world. Let's make it happen!

I wanted to share this quote that is very dear to my heart. It was given to me by one of my closest and most treasured friends. Without this friend I would not be where I am today, since I had such limiting beliefs and thought I was a nothing. Through believing in God and the people He sends our way, I now believe I am special and that made all the difference in the world.

If I could give you one gift, I would give you the ability to see yourself as I see you, so you could see how truly special you are.

—Unknown

Chapter 1

Escaping the Shelf

"Being put on the shelf is just one way to say you are no longer useful in this world and whatever the unique gift was that God gave you has never been unwrapped."

—Pat Pilla

One terrible day, my father informed me that no one would want me and that I would be a "thing" someone would put on a shelf.

I stared at him in rising anger, tears streaming uncontrollably down my cheeks and onto the floor. My hands clenched with hatred and my body became stiff. I thought to myself, "How can my own father say that to me?" My mind went numb. I was shattered beyond words. I ran into my bedroom, slamming the door behind me.

I felt degraded and worthless. This one statement from my father would prove to have a lasting impact on me. That day was the lowest of lows in my life.

I was 15 years old and obese. I lacked any control over myself, my life, and my future. My father's words rang so true to me at that time that they became embedded in my mind. And that is where they remained. Every time I doubted myself, those words came back, and rang true to me. I was a "thing."

I struggled to love myself, to feel worthy, but it never seemed to work. How could I love myself when my own father didn't love me? I never felt loved, so how could I give love? It is hard to imagine that a parent could say such heartless words to his child, without hesitation.

That was my father. He worked two jobs to support my mom and 5 kids and that was his top priority. My mother hardly ever went out of the house, so my father did all the shopping and outings.

When I think about it, I'm amazed that I managed to attain a life - a real life - and survive.

What helped me was my ability to see a person's sensitive side, even when they were being mean. At a young age, I discovered that people were often nasty because they were hurting inside   - just like I was - and that is how they coped with the pain. Although my father would say harsh things to me, he would take me shopping and fishing out on Coney Island, or take me to the Bronx Zoo. He had a good heart, but hid it beneath his own insecurities.

Tears still spring to my eyes when I think of what my father said to me. Words affect each one of us; no matter how hard we try, we never seem to forget the cruel ones. Something bad happens and bingo, you are back to reliving the way you felt that very day and moment. I worked through many torturous years to get where I am today. Thinking back and looking at myself now, I have to say, "WOW, baby, you came a long way!"

I struggled with my weight throughout my life. I did all the fads - the diets, pills, fake foods - you name it, I tried it. I came to realize that it was me who had to change, but my attitude was stopping me. If I felt unworthy, why would I want to help myself?

Prayer and a sense of self-worth changed my entire mindset and put me on the path to recovery. God doesn't make junk. I was special and I was loved. That knowledge is what held me together, and I live by that today.

So – Dad, you were totally wrong. I am not a trinket or a thing on a shelf, sitting around, getting dusty. I got plucked from that freakin' shelf. I got married. I have a wonderful daughter and son-in-law, and two beautiful grandsons. I have been truly blessed with awesome family and friends. I have a great career and opened my own business. Hey, I even got on TV!!!

I am a woman with a soul and a life that is worth living.

Amazingly, the "Shelf" incident made me stronger. I became sensitive to people and nonjudgmental of others. I have compassion for all the so-called misfits that enter my world. I appreciate their pain and struggles. With those terrible words, my father taught me a lesson about humanity and I thank him for that:

Thank you, Dad, for teaching me about life, even though you didn't know that you did. You molded me into the person I am today and I am grateful for that. Because of you, I see the good in everyone I meet. You taught me how to be sensitive and caring; to always say a nice word to people and cheer them up on a bad day.

You see Dad, I have a heart like you, but I choose to show it on my sleeve instead of hiding it and becoming bitter like you did. I live with compassion and love, and I not only forgive you for that day, I am eternally grateful to you.

What you should take away from this is to never let anyone's words become your law, especially your Evil Twin. The people who criticize you are struggling with insecurity, not you. We are molded by our experiences and keeping that internal hope alive is the thing that makes a difference.

I will show you how to start living the life that was meant for you, a life that burns with passion and has dignity. You will finally jump the *hell* off that shelf, unwrap that gift, and share your superpower with the world. I know how because I was there.

"To all the so called "misfits" out there: If you follow your path, eventually you will reach a destination where no one else has been. You are meant for a unique purpose that only belongs to you."

—Pat Pilla

CHAPTER 2

Living Your Life Purpose

"The purpose of life is not to be happy. It is to be useful, to be honorable, to be compassionate, to have it make some difference that you have lived and lived well."

—Ralph Waldo Emerson

We often wrestle with these questions: Why am I here? What is my true purpose in this huge world? Isn't there a more positive direction for my life?

These questions can echo in our minds. I honestly think they are supernaturally planted in our subconscious the day we are conceived. We look around to see what others are doing. We may dabble in various jobs and hobbies, but seem to come up short. We know deep down that we are not living up to our potential, that there must be more. We can't possibly be born into this vast world and just exist. No way! It is a difficult task to find the answer to your own existence in a world full of uncertainty and pressure.

We were all created with a distinct purpose - we exist to make a difference. No one is the same. You have a unique gift, rooted in your soul, which radiates throughout your body. Most of us keep it so safely tucked away that we forget about our gift; we are so caught up in our daily routines, we even forget about our purpose. That gift gets thrown on a shelf, to be saved for a rainy day, when we have time to open it.

Instead of tapping into that inner power, we start listening to the outside world, or to others who think they "know better," who want to keep us safe. By doing this, we lose who we are and allow ourselves to be molded into what they want of us, instead of who we want to be.

Why do we do this? Is it insecurity, fear, or is it that we don't value our own opinions of ourselves?

After years of agonizing attempts, I realized that I did not understand my true calling in life. My vision of helping young people was overshadowed by my hobbies, my "stuff," and misguided goals. Hobbies and goals are not the same as your vision. A vision is your gift, the one thing that sets your soul on fire with a flame that never smolders. This is a God-given gift that only you have. No one on this planet possesses what you have. We all have our own unique flair. Your potential is your DNA, it's who you are.

I once mentored a young woman named Rosa. Rosa was just starting out in a new business venture and she was beginning to express herself. She had deprived herself of her dreams because of fear and self-doubt that paralyzed her from moving forward. I needed to help Rosa find her superpower! What spark did she need to ignite to set that fire? After only a few sessions together, Rosa was able to fully see that her self-imposed, self-limiting beliefs were destroying her, and her evil twin was undermining her. She kept to her comfort zone for far too long, and as we worked together, Rosa was finally able to break free and find her true potential.

Her journey resonated with me every step of the way because I had done the same thing. I would start a venture and when it didn't go right or the way I wanted, I would quit, thinking that I wasn't good enough or that someone wouldn't like it. I was always worried about other people's opinions. That was my evil twin at work, lurking behind my subconscious and attacking me. It took many years to deaden that nasty twin's voice.

Your true life's purpose is designed for you alone. You were uniquely and wonderfully made. Once I knew that, I began to search high and low for my gift, or my superpower. I studied people who loved what they did. No matter what it was, they were glowing. Their energy level was through the roof and you could see their total fulfillment. Fire ablaze, their gifts were being used for a higher purpose.

I found that these people were living their passion. They had a definite purpose and they were living fully and without regret. They also knew which tasks were important to them, and which weren't. Though the road was bumpy at times, they never lost their main vision: their purpose became a beacon of light. Keeping their purpose in sight created an endless surge of energy to forge ahead and achieve their vision.

I also noticed that when you're living your purpose, it's not about money. People who found their purpose would do what they were blessed to do for free. In a sense, money has no purpose in your purpose. Of course, you need money to survive. But when you live in your God-given gift, money will come. Even so, money should not be the "Why" to your purpose.

As you can see, people who chase money are never satisfied. They want more and more and their bank accounts can never be big enough. Chasing material things will not make you happy. Yes, it may make you comfortable, but it will never make you as happy as living your purpose and serving others. We were not created to chase money.

A purposeful life gives you direction. As you nurture your gift, you'll feel a sense of accomplishment. Keep your life purpose well nourished by always putting your best foot forward and trying to serve.

When you give to others what you possess within your soul, the joy you experience cannot be explained. Sharing your talents is priceless. We were born to serve; that seems to be the golden nugget in the scheme of living your purpose and a life that is totally fulfilled. When your soul is on fire, people resonate with you and you become contagious. People will want what you have; little do they know they already have exactly what they need inside of themselves. In looking inward to your soul, not outward to the world and its distractions, you will find your purpose.

Finding Your Purpose

Tap into close friends and family and ask them, "What is the one thing that stands out when you think of me?" People who know you well will see the potential in you that you don't usually see in yourself. Remember though, they may be pointing out your hobbies and not your real purpose, but it's a great starting point to reflect upon.

You will also find your gift as you begin to search your soul. It's right there. All you have to do is tap into it. Be still and sit quietly. As you remain in your quiet place ask yourself, "What is my purpose? Why are I here?" You will start to hear a calm inner voice, faintly at first, whispering the answers that your sub-conscience has been holding back.

As you continue to think of things that you love to do, the voice will gain power and strength, and explode into a shout. Go with the flow and continue to think of all the things you love to do. Feel yourself fill with excitement and joy.

As you continue to fill your mind with those things you love, the voice will get louder and that whisper will explode like dynamite. You will get so excited that tears will stream down your face and you will think of nothing else. This is your gift. This is your superpower. Unwrap it!

Be who and what you were created to be. Be YOU and let no one stop you from experiencing that desire.

Don't ever give up on your gift because you would be robbing the world of You, and you will be denying God the gift he placed in your heart.

If you are constantly wondering, "Who am I?" you can use these strategies that I put together to help you find your purpose and visualize the steps to your goals; they have helped me find my truest potential and I want to share them with you:

Sit quietly alone in a room. No distractions, no electronics, just pure silence. The focus is on you, your thoughts, and tapping into your inner soul.

Close your eyes and let your mind wander. Think of the things that you love to do. Don't worry what it is; think of everything you love. It can be school, art, music, sports - even walking your dog - whatever you love, let it flow within your mind.

Think of some things that you use to do as a child that gave you joy.

What makes you alive and energized?

When have you been the happiest in your life?

Ask yourself, "How will this serve the greater good of the world?"

Don't rush while answering these questions. Take it nice and slow and continue to sit peacefully.

When you step out of the zone, open your eyes. Write down what you said to yourself during the meditation, and start by setting small goals to reach your vision. Get yourself uncomfortable being comfortable! Each baby step you take out of your comfort zone will be leaps towards your superpower.

After you have ignited that spark, look for mentors/coaches and people that share your vision. Follow and learn from them and avoid activities that distract you from your purpose.

As you write these words down on paper, they become valid. Your eyes will open up to the many aspects of your life's purpose and you can start prioritizing them and take the necessary steps to implement their purpose.

Once you pare down your more specific purpose, you can write up an action plan on how you are going to achieve it. Stay the course and develop small goals, taking steps each day that will propel you towards accomplishing your dream.

Here are my tips for Setting Goals 101:

> ➤ First and foremost, believe in yourself. This is crucial to building a foundation. If you build a house on a weak foundation, it will crumble. Give yourself a rock-solid base to build upon. Believe in yourself and others will, too.

> ➤ Write your goal(s) on a piece of paper. Create a completion date for each goal; for example, 6 months, 12 months, etc. Visualize the steps you need to take action on and plot them on your timeline. Visualizing these steps in your mind is like seeing a recipe. You can see the completed recipe, but you also need to follow the steps in order to create the final delicious outcome. There are ingredients and there are steps you need to take right at this moment to obtain your goal(s). Reaching a goal is a step-by-step process.

> ➤ Give a list of goals to an accountability partner; that is, someone who has an unbiased opinion and understands what you are striving for, and a person who will keep you accountable on a weekly basis as you make progress.

Accountability partners might also be someone you trust to offer various ideas, insights, and advice. Pay attention to them, especially if they are at a point in their business or life where you would like to be.

➢ Goals will not be reached by thinking about them or dreaming about them. You have to take action. You will go encounter many obstacles and doors that may slam shut in your face. Keep pushing forward and don't get discouraged. Being discouraged never serves anyone. Strive and stay positive. There are going to be unforeseen obstacles, so get used to it!

➢ Motivation and consistency are vital to making progress. Reward yourself for each goal reached.

➢ Get a calendar and mark it up with non-negotiable steps to obtain each goal. Try to accomplish one thing at a time. We were not designed to be a multi-tasker. Focus on the most important to the least important task and take it step by step.

➢ Create an environment that encourages you to stay focused. I created a woman's cave for me. I go into that cave and I am centered and focused as soon as I walk in. This is my happy place.

➢ Always stay true to your life purpose because even though your goals may change, you have to make sure your life purpose is true to you. That is what is going to keep that fire burning in your soul and sustain you through the hardships.

➢ It's important that you gather a network of friends and family that are going to encourage you along the way. Seek out like-minded people that will push you and support when things get difficult. If you can, hire a coach who has been there and is willing to steer you in the right direction. Stay away from people who try to sabotage you and your dream. Keep a positive mindset that will guide you throughout your journey and remember to serve, serve, serve, and always live your life with purpose.

Chapter 3

Comfort

"Comfort zones are comfortable because they're familiar, not because they're healthy."

—Craig Groeschel

As young children, we were so carefree; life was easy. There were no decisions to make; we were fed, bathed, and clothed. We did whatever we wanted and our young minds were intensely curious about the world around us. We had a need to know, to touch, and to understand. Our eyes were filled with excitement and we couldn't wait for the next adventure to happen. It's extraordinary to see things for the first time; as they say, though the eyes of a child.

As I started writing this book, it made me wonder why I couldn't bring back those days. Why can't I see with the awe-filled eyes of a child seeing everything for the first time? Why?

As we grow up and leave our childish world behind us, we quickly learn what is wrong, what is right, and what is expected from us. If that's not enough, we start to doubt our very own existence. When you are born, your mind is a clean slate; gradually it gets chalked up with other people's ideas and beliefs. Life can become cloudy and leave you feeling disoriented.

We were good and listened to our parents, friends and others who told us what to do with our lives. They wanted us to live the life they lived, albeit not a very happy one, but one that was safe and secure. "Security" was the answer for everyone that held back on their vision, depriving themselves and the world of their gift in the process. It becomes a never-ending cycle until someone steps up to the plate and rattles our existence. You need courage and a strong belief in yourself to tear yourself out of this "safe' life. It also takes persistence and fortitude to be able run with what we believe we were meant to do.

We often second-guess ourselves because of the opposition we get from the outside world. That is when our "evil twin" pokes its devious head out at us. When you start believing your evil twin's lies, fear sets in and you can start to second-guess your own intuition. That chalk gets so thick that it obscures your purpose. Instead of realizing your gift, it becomes easier to seek comfort ... comfort that was taught by others so we can remain safe. Comfort plays a strong role in our evil twin's game, a role that eventually smothers your soul.

There is the one thing to remember; you are never safe as long as your evil twin continues to lurk in your subconscious mind. You can say to yourself, "I can," but your evil twin will whisper, "You can't." Your evil twin will hold you back as if in chains, keeping you from growing, and keeping you complacent. He plants the seed in your mind - as long as you are safe and secure, you are fine. This is a lie.

I am going to show you how you can wipe that slate clean, because it's time to live the life you were created to live.

Discipline

"Someday" and "later" are the most deceiving words in the English vocabulary, and of the evil twin. "Someday" will never come and neither will "later" if you don't discipline yourself to move towards your goals. Self-discipline is one of the keys to success.

How many times do you go to work to a job that you just don't like? A job that sometimes you blatantly hate? Sunday night comes rolling around and you get a sick feeling in your gut. Monday morning is tomorrow - and here you go again - another week of misery. You know you are not living up to your superpower, but you remain in that dreaded job. Why??

I'll tell you why! You are too comfortable and secure. Exactly like you were told when you were younger, and now your evil twin keeps reminding you of it. Safe and secure; safe and secure; he whispers it over and over again.

You need to take a leap of faith and get out of that situation. If you remain complacent, and choose comfort, you will never grow.

I am reminded of an incident that happened to me at a prior job. Over thirty years ago, I briefly worked for an overseas shipping company. My job was to make sure the commodities were being shipped smoothly. This also meant that I had to track all air and sea shipments from the states to their destinations all over the world and make sure the currency for each country was correct. To say I hated this job is an understatement. Also, our boss smoked and we were not allowed to open the windows for air. When he walked into a room, it was as if all of us ceased to breathe and exist. I never worked in a place where everyone was afraid of the boss. I felt like I was on another planet. Can you imagine grown people being afraid to speak to or even look at their superior?

While I was there, I met a girl named Sara. I told her that I had to get out of this job and she said, "You are making good money here and you will NEVER find another job that will pay you so much per hour, which is why I stay here." At the time, I was earning $12 per hour. I looked at her in shock over what she was saying to me.

When Sara told me that I would never earn more than what I was paid in this crap hole of a company, it sent shivers down my spine. I knew I had to quit. Yet I felt sad for Sara, who thought this was the best she could do. Imagine a young girl not believing she was worthy of more than that. I'm sure I was meant to meet Sara; she got me so fired up that I quit, secured another job that more than doubled my pay, but also showed me that I was worthy of so much more.

Sara's evil twin was working on her – and she lived in fear; the fear of having nothing or the fact that she felt she was unworthy of anything else. Even though Sara did not like her job, she stayed there for security. A sure bet! She was comfortable.

OVERCOMING YOUR EVIL TWIN

Always remember that your evil twin will be prowling around your mind, waiting for a chance to resurface. The more in control you are of the goals you've set to reach your vision, the safer you will be. By shrinking your comfort zone, you are actually expanding your growth and becoming more unstoppable each and every day. Let fear work for you, not against you.

If you are feeling anxious or stressed, your distress is being caused by staying in that comfort zone! The bigger it is, the more lifeless you will feel.

You have built a space in your subconscious where there are boundaries and security. Believe me, you are not going to get anywhere with keeping the status quo. Your evil twin is all about keeping you comfortable. Why use your full potential when you can stay wrapped up in comfort, and never have to leave that warm and fuzzy spot? Because humans need growth! We need to evolve and grow into our potential even if it means getting a bit dirty and uncomfortable.

Here are a few tips for you to get past the limits of your comfort zone and expand your potential:

✓ Do something every day that scares the crap out of you.

- ✓ Make a list and jot down EVERYTHING you are fearful of; i.e. money, health, relationships, career, etc. Then, break down the steps to facing each fear.

- ✓ Examine what you are afraid of. Ask yourself, are you looking inward and getting self-absorbed.

- ✓ Are you allowing your past to be in your present? Did you not heal or let go of those memories that you thought were gone.

- ✓ Are you still making your past dominate how you feel and allowing your fears to take over which is not the truth?

- ✓ Give yourself permission to fail.

- ✓ Reward yourself for every accomplishment towards breaking down those fears.

- ✓ Try being kinder and less harsh with yourself.

- ✓ Accept that you are less than perfect.

- ✓ Let go of your expectations and accept the results of your actions.

- ✓ Be open-minded and be more daring.

OVERCOMING YOUR EVIL TWIN

- ✓ Stand up to your fears. Break them down and seek the truth in each situation.

- ✓ Don't let the boundaries that live in your mental space take over and destroy your destiny.

Chapter 4

Comparison: Self-Doubt & your Evil Twin

"Comparison is the death of joy."

—Mark Twain

Research has found that comparing ourselves to others propagates feelings of envy, low self-confidence, and depression, as well as compromising our ability to trust others. Self-comparison is damaging to your sense of self.

When I compared myself with my peers, I would get so down on myself. I imagined they had the magic bullet. I felt these people were born under a lucky star and I had nothing. It was a pity party in my head almost every day. I thought I did enough. I thought I had it all together. So, "Why is this happening to me?" Here we go again - the Evil Twin is back.

Comparison limits you from your full potential. Comparing yourself to someone else paralyzes you with feelings of worthlessness, so you give up on your dreams. You may say to yourself, "I can never be like them," or "Why can't I get ahead?" or "I deserve it; I work just as hard as they do." Does this sound familiar to you??

Did you ever start on a new venture/hobby and knew the moment you started it that this was definitely for you. You loved every part of it. The planning; the design; the networking. You were on fire! You worked day-in and day-out. You had big dreams and then one day the fire smoldered, you became exhausted and couldn't even catch your breath. The spark was gone like a puff of smoke.

You tried so many things to get yourself on the right foot, but no matter what you tried it never seemed to click. You started looking at other people and would ask yourself, "Why can't I do what they are doing?" or "Why did it work for them and not for me?" The "Whys" become huge. Those words smacked you across your face. You kept on comparing yourself to others and finding yourself lacking.

Do not compare yourself to anyone – that only wastes time in developing who you really are. You are always looking outside of yourself for permission on whether you are good or not, and your Evil Twin preys heavily on this. Each of us holds a special place in this world. We are not cloned, so why compare? Just be YOU!

Develop your craft and make it work for you and you alone. Look to others for guidance, but never to compare. Everyone walks their own path and you do not need to follow their footsteps. Make your own path and make that path glow as each step illuminates the way to your vision. Shine brightly the way you were supposed to shine. Did you ever notice that people in the same field do things so much differently than each other? That is because they are unique.

As we take steps to begin to acknowledge what has happened in our life and why our fires burn out, we need to realize that maybe this was a part of a journey to take us to the next level.

Self-doubt is the killer of dreams. Instead use this as a tool to move you past a difficult patch in your life. Pause and reflect on those dreams and desires that fuel your heart and keep you moving in the most difficult times.

Focus on your achievements and accomplishments instead of your deficiencies. Work on your gift, the areas that set your soul on fire.

"Encourage yourself, believe in yourself, and love yourself. Never doubt who you are."

—Stephanie Lahart

Strategies to Self-Love

How do I get rid of my self-limiting beliefs, you ask? First and foremost, you must love yourself. I don't mean in an egotistical, narcissistic way; I mean really love who you are. You truly are the best thing that ever happened to you. Now give yourself a big hug and enjoy that gift that you are!

Once you fully love yourself, and appreciate who you are, the self-limiting beliefs that you imposed on yourself start to diminish and so does your evil twin. The best way I found to love myself is to be one with my soul. I am who I am and I am loved. It is so simple, yet we make it so complex. We need to take better care of the house in which we were created. That house is our body, where our spirit lives and thrives. We need to take care of it and nurture it as much as possible. That body gives us the stamina to go on. When our body is healthy and vibrant, we feel unstoppable.

Why do we have such a tough time trying to love ourselves? We have a tendency to take a back seat. Always remember you are a treasure, a priceless being that should be loved and nurtured. You don't have to listen to the outside world to know the beauty that is inside of you. Your spirit is a light to those around you and it shines so radiantly. You are God's masterpiece.

Here are some steps you can follow to get your mojo back up and running. Remember, this is only the beginning of the beautiful life you have to offer to others and to yourself as well.

❖ Acknowledge the fact that you are comparing yourself to others. If you don't acknowledge you cannot change. Be aware, because awareness is key!

❖ Focus on what you have. Once you realize that comparing yourself to others doesn't work in your favor, you'll look for additional measures of your success.

- ❖ Spend more of your time focusing on the positive and good in your life. You may find that you start noticing more of it when you're not busy comparing yourself to others.

- ❖ Keep a gratitude journal. A gratitude journal is a way to remind yourself of what you have. Appreciate what you do have in this very moment and continue to feel that pleasure in knowing that you are loved and that you are love.

- ❖ Don't take things for granted. They can be taken away from you at any moment.

- ❖ Replace your negative thoughts with positive ones. Keep a list close by of all your wonderful qualities so when those nasty thoughts come to play you have the positive ones to replace them with.

- ❖ Don't envy anyone with regard to what their talents are. You have your own talents, so nurture them.

- ❖ Make decisions based on what you want to do, not what everyone else wants you to do.

❖ Improve and work on your own abilities. If you do feel lack in a certain area, learn more about it. Educate yourself because knowledge is key in growing and gaining more confidence.

❖ Compete with yourself and not others to reach higher goals. Appreciate others instead of envying them.

❖ Take the risk and get out of your comfort zone. You can be assured that once you take risks you are at a different level entirely. Taking risks builds your self-confidence ten-fold.

❖ In a journal, write down how you view yourself, and any thoughts or feelings that come to mind. As you write these thoughts and feeling down, take note what is really true and what is really false. Ask people in your inner circle how they view you. Become very aware of your thoughts about yourself because most likely these thoughts are stories that you have been telling yourself for years and are not true at all.

❖ Set goals for yourself that will build your confidence.

❖ Always know that comparing yourself to others will have a negative impact on you. By using these strategies and acknowledging how comparing yourself makes you feel, you will be more successful in changing that negative behavior.

The only real way to quiet your negative emotions and forget about what was upsetting you is to fill your time with a positive action. Make it a fun distraction. Suppressing or analyzing those negative thoughts will not be as effective. Put on some music and dance like no one is watching!

You were born to shine and we all have a purpose. Your dreams do matter to all of us in this vast world. Without you we would be one less heartbeat from changing the world and we would all suffer. You're that important and that special.

Chapter 5

It's Your Choice

"Attitude is a choice. Happiness is a choice. Optimism is a choice. Kindness is a choice. Giving is a choice. Respect is a choice. Whatever choice you make makes you. Choose wisely."

—Roy T. Bennett

We all have the gift of choice. We ALL have full freedom to choose what we do and say. The same way we are careful with what we put into our bodies, we should be ultra-careful about what we put into our minds. Feed your mind the same way you feed your body. Nourish it well and good things will pour out. If you put junk into your body, you will be afflicted by disease. It's the same with your mind; try to keep it as healthy as possible with positive energy, not negative garbage.

How many people do you know who cling to their problems? They are a dime a dozen, don't you think?

Why do you think they cling? Is it because they lack attention? Or do they just love to talk about themselves and how miserable they are? They crave sympathy for every misfortune that occurred to them from the time they were born and they express their agony and turmoil to everyone they come in contact with. Warning! Warning! Stay away from this type of person. They will drag you down. These people don't even want to try to overcome their Evil Twin. They love where they are; they are comfortable in their own doom and gloom. This type of behavior is extremely toxic.

I had people like this in my life. I tried to help by being sympathetic and understanding, and tried hard to meet their needs, but their needs are never met because they love living in that place of self-sabotage and pain.

We all have a choice to be happy. Happiness seems to be the key word at the moment. Everyone wants to be happy. Happiness is the end all, be all!

First and foremost, I want to set you straight. You cannot - repeat after me - **cannot** be happy 100% of the time. That is not realistic, and if you think it is, you are setting yourself up for major pain. Life is not always sugar and spice. I have been living on this earth for a long time and there have been great moments where I was so happy, my heart would sing – as a matter of fact, I have been on cloud nine. There were also moments where my heart hurt so bad it felt like it was broken. This is a normal course of life for all of us.

I don't want you to have this strange notion that you should be happy 100% of the time, because believe it or not you are putting this negative thought right into your mind. Trying to strive for happiness all the time will make you miserable. You will always think that you are not doing enough, or others are not enough to make you happy. In reality, you are enough!

Happiness is a state of mind. It depends on how you deal with the negative aspects of your life. You can take a situation that is difficult and make yourself miserable over it, or you can take the same situation, and with a different mindset, create a happy outcome. We have the choice to wallow in it and suffer, or move on and let it go. It's your choice to stay in your negative state of mind; but the question is, "How is that serving you?"

Think of all of the things that make you grateful. Be grateful for being alive; for getting up in the morning and seeing the sun shining. Praise the fact that you are living and breathing. Applaud each and every day that you have been given to take another chance, to try a little harder, to make a difference in someone's life. Act selflessly and serve others. This is where your true happiness lies.

Look for the positive in people. Even if they aren't kind to you – you never know what is happening in a person's life.

A long time ago, I would walk past the same girl at church every Sunday. She ignored me as if I was invisible. It infuriated me. I felt if I physically knocked her down, she would still not see me. My evil twin was lurking and I began to think of all the reasons why she ignored me. I spoke to my Pastor at the time about it and his answer was not the one I was looking for. He told me that I had to change! Well, talk about being infuriated. He told me that everyone has issues and that I should go up to her and say hello.

After I calmed down, a couple of weeks later, she did it again. This time, I took her aside and asked her if I offended her and why every time I passed her, she always ignored me. She was shocked. She didn't have a clue what I was talking about. I found out that she was having problems with her family, her job, and her health - she didn't even realize I was there.

From that moment on, we greeted each other with open arms.

Don't listen to your evil twin and don't make erroneous assumptions like I did. Be kind and make a choice to change and act differently.

Chapter 6

Respect Yourself

"You should not measure your own qualities in regard to the qualities of some other person. Respect yourself just the way you are."

—Ruben Papian

We were taught by our parents and our teachers that we must respect one another and we must "talk nicely" to people. We were taught manners and how to behave. The one thing we were never taught was how to talk to and treat ourselves.

Don't you think we should speak to ourselves like we were taught to speak to others? Shouldn't we be treating

49

ourselves with respect, the way we were taught to treat others?

Well, since we were never taught that, I want you to start talking nicely to yourself!

YES! You are so worthy.

Don't let negative messages into your brain. With just a few simple words, like "I can't do that," "I don't know how," "I'll never succeed," you are sabotaging yourself. These phrases are silently prowling around your mind and when you repeat them, you make them fact.

When you say *"I can't,"* believe me, you won't. Instead say more positive words like *"I can," "I will," "I know,"* etc. Get out of that old rut of talking to yourself in the negative.

I know those negative phrases flow freely out of your mouth before you even know you're saying them. Your subconscious mind remembers and those pessimistic words stick in there like glue.

Treat yourself with respect, the way you were taught to treat others; otherwise, how should you expect others to respect you? We hold on to certain values that should not be tainted by anyone. No one will take away your values and respect unless you allow it. Once you decide to give in to something you don't believe in, whether it is personal or business, you've crossed a line. Now, you've allowed others into your circle that may not take you seriously, or know that you can be coerced. You've lost your power and you've lost your self-respect. It's your job to hold on to your values even if you have to stand alone. We all want to fit in, but at the end of the day, is It really worth it?

"Great values are built on strong moral foundations. Men become great when they allow these values to take root within their souls and live by them."

—Lincoln Patz

Feed your mind positive food. You are enough and you already have what you need inside of you, so stop the daily crap talk to yourself and change your mind set to where your "soul set" is.

Not only will you live a fulfilled and better life, you will be happier knowing that you are talking to yourself with the respect that you deserve. My teaching was always to treat others the same way that you would like to be treated, and that my dear friend is a mouthful. But don't forget to also treat *yourself* the way you treat others. That means no negative talk because you are the first one who hears your voice.

Be careful what you say to yourself. Your subconscious hears everything and takes in the negativity - and it won't let it go until you make yourself fully aware of what you're doing and stop it dead in its tracks.

I hope this helps you out and that you talk to yourself with true dignity and respect because you deserve it.

Chapter 7

Fear – Friend or Foe?

"Too many of us are not living our dreams because we are living our fears."

—Les Brown

Don't operate in fear. You don't have to fear anything, Do what God put in your soul and use wisdom to do the best you can. Fear is not your friend.

Without dreams and goals, you will never see greatness in your life. Those gifts that have been instilled in you will die and be buried with the rest of your unfulfilled dreams. What a shame to rob us all of your potential.

Believe it or not, Failure is our FRIEND! First of all, I want to say that failures in our life are learning experiences. Very few of us, if any, succeed without having failures.

Each person reacts differently to failure, but the major setbacks for most people are similar. It could be a failed job, an unhappy marriage or a failed business venture. You have to get over the trauma. A setback is a shock to your system.

Setbacks are a difficult experience because when they occur, we are left vulnerable and open to negative emotions. The more that a setback feels like a failure, the more likely it is to keep its grip on you. You become more wary of risk, sometimes to a point of anxiety. There are feelings of guilt and possibly shame that can lead to anger and fear.

You start to obsesses, and that inner critic - our Evil Twin - will speak up and say, "What did I do wrong?" Or you'll hear victim-mode question Number One, "Why did this happen to me?"

We hate to fail. We fear it; we dread it, and when it happens we tend to hold on to it. We can give it power over our emotions and sometimes we allow it to dictate our way forward.

"If you live in fear of the future because of what happened in your past, you'll end up losing what you have in the present."

—Nishan Panwar

Personal setbacks take time to heal so you have to give yourself room to grieve. Don't hide from your pain, because denial makes healing take longer. We need to let go and forgive ourselves and move on.

Don't spend too much time with the "What ifs." Instead, find someone who's had a similar experience to help you. Tackle your vision of the future in a positive way. Don't take it to heart. Separate the setback from your identity. Just because you haven't found a successful way to accomplish this yet, that doesn't mean you are a failure. Personalizing failure can destroy your self-esteem and confidence. Do not let your failures define you.

Stop dwelling on it. Obsessing over your setback or failure will only bring you more misery. It will not change the outcome. It's done and dwelling on it will stop you from moving forward. The quicker you take positive action, the less debilitating it will be.

Setbacks can make you question your self-worth, your goals and your future. That fear of failure may limit you, leaving you nervous to face the next steps. My own fear of failure was that I was going to be judged or lose respect. Remember, don't be influenced by anyone; this is your life, not theirs.

What one person considers to be true about you is not necessarily the truth. Don't give too much power to other's opinions. Did you know that Oprah was fired from her first TV job where she was co-anchor of the 6 pm news at WJZ-TV in Baltimore? WJZ decided she was dull and stiff on the air and noted she regularly mispronounced words. Walt Disney was fired from his newspaper job because they said he lacked imagination and good ideas. There are many great people that also failed at one point; talk about failing forward!!!

Recovery from a setback isn't the same for everyone. Those who are crushed will internalize it as "I'm a failure"; some are at the opposite end of the spectrum and thrive on stress, only to fight harder when they go down. That is where I am.

After years of setbacks, nothing is going to get me down. I pick myself up and move forward. Instead of saying to myself, "If I fail it means that I am stupid, weak, or incapable and I am never going to make it," I altered my thinking pattern. I take a positive approach and say, "If I fail, I am one step closer to succeeding. I am smarter and wiser because of the knowledge I've gained through this experience."

I don't play games. With the time I waste feeling sorry for myself, I could be more constructive and positive towards getting myself back up. Instead of feeling sorry for myself, I help others who are in need. It gives me a chance to get out of my own head, and in helping others, I realize that my life is not that bad. Of course, I'm human and I have feelings that get hurt, but I have learned that setbacks are there to make us stronger. Though it's a hell of a way to make us stronger, I also believe that we need to experience setbacks and failures in order to appreciate what we have and how far we've come. They bring us back to who we are so we can regroup and move forward. I have learned true life lessons from them. It is extremely important to share your setbacks and that you aren't ashamed of them. We all have them whether you like it or not.

You have the choice to keep yourself centered. Again, I talk about choice!! CHOICE is what we all have. You need to bring yourself back to who you are and what you are trying to achieve. A self-confident person doesn't usually fear the ups and downs of their world, because they created a strong foundation in who they are. Tap into your faith and dig deep into who you are and why you are here.

Instead of calling it a failure, call it a learning experience. It can take a setback to make us see that some of our habits are not that productive and that we have to re-focus and re-tweak them.

I recognize my setbacks and I bounce my ideas off of others to gain insight. As painful as it may be to suffer a setback, recognize that you can go on. I accept responsibility for my setback and as I said, I made choices that led me to that setback. Now I try to make better choices in the future and I ask myself, "What can I do differently?"

I have also become more knowledgeable. When I have a setback, I learn from it. My experience allows me to change direction. That leads us to the next question, "What direction?" I pray and calm myself down, and then try to figure out where it went wrong. I ask questions and have a mentor help on to the next step. You can also ask someone who is also like-minded who have the same interests and research some of their ideas and strategies.

I persevere, too! When Thomas Edison was working on the light bulb, he reportedly failed 10,000 times. I can hardly imagine what he went through, especially the negativity from his own peers. He was quoted as saying "I have found 10,000 ways something won't work. I am not discouraged, because every wrong attempt discarded is another step forward." What an incredible man. He surely believed in himself and in his vision, and that gave him the power to push onward through numerous failures. In reality, each time he failed he was getting closer to being successful. Failing may mean that you have to change your behavior in ways that will lead to success, without giving up on your vision.

Most of us go to great lengths to avoid failure due to the fear and shame associated with it. People who are close to you can actually see the behaviors that may have led to your failure more clearly than you can. They may see the strengths, too, that will help you rise above it. Take heed and listen carefully to their feedback. We are never too old or too young to learn.

While a setback can seem devastating, it can also serve as an opportunity. Our failures make us interesting people and help us to obtain wisdom. They teach us to see life more clearly and allow us to cope more effectively with the problems that life sends our way. If you expect setbacks or failures, you won't be devastated when they happen.

Personally, I have "me" time and pray to God to thank Him for every challenge He sends my way. I know that together we will get through it and that helps me to find peace.

Overcoming Setbacks

Ultimately, the ability to deal with setbacks is at the heart of a successful and happy person. It's extremely helpful to set goals, so you can see the direction you need to go in the future.

Remember, failures are separate from your personality. A failure is not your identity. Personalizing it will wreck your self-esteem and confidence and send you spiraling down an unhappy path. Don't worry about what people are thinking about your so called failure. It doesn't matter.

Stop dwelling on your failure. God created eyes in front of your head so there is no looking back. You can't change the past, but you can shape the future. The sooner you realize this, the faster you will be able to forge ahead.

See the failure for exactly what it is and accept responsibility; find out why it happened. Gather facts and make a list. What can you change to move yourself forward?

Here are a few tips to help you along:

➤ Do NOT take your failures personally.

➤ Let go of the need to seek approval from others.

➤ See the failure/setback for what it really is.

- ➤ Talk it over with your closest people and get feedback from them.

- ➤ Write a list of things that you did and what can be changed for a more positive outcome.

- ➤ Forgive yourself.

Michael Jordan nailed it when he said, "I have missed more than 9,000 shots in my career. I have lost almost 300 games. On 26 occasions I have been entrusted to take the game winning shot, and I missed. I have failed over and over and over again in my life. And that is why I succeeded."

"Most great people have attained their greatest success just one step beyond their greatest failure."

—Napoleon Hill

Chapter 8

Focus

"One of the greatest regrets in life is being what others would want you to be, rather than being yourself.

—**Shannon L. Alder**

Where your focus goes, energy flows. Unless you focus on your goals and take action there can be no growth, because action needs focused energy to survive. Without focus, you become complacent and your goals will die along with your dreams. Focus on your dreams and start unwrapping the gift that has been inside you since birth.

OVERCOMING YOUR EVIL TWIN

You DESERVE your dream so turn down the negativity, shut out that Evil Twin, and rev up the positivity. Let's take action, because ALL action starts with YOU!

Many people don't value their gifts. They may feel that they are not worthy of sharing. By not sharing your gifts to the world, you are robbing it of your greatness. I cannot stress that enough! We *all* have greatness within us!

Your Number One question to yourself should be, "How can I serve the world with my talents?" You will see that serving others is the best job in town and you can also earn a living by doing it. You can apply your gifts to the world and help others realize their greatness too. It becomes a circle of love. That is why the greatest gift on earth is LOVE!

When you start working towards your goal, recognize your own value and see what can be possible in the next week, the next month and in the next year. Take small steps that will bring you closer to your goal. Mentor with a person who loves the same things you do, and continue to associate with people that push you instead of dragging you down.

We *all* need help and guidance. You cannot do it alone. See how you can maximize your inner circle and build a solid foundation with like-minded ambitious people like you. Establish relationships that make you soar, not only in your field of expertise, but also in your personal life as well.

Keep the faith that all things are possible and that you have all that is needed right inside of you. Celebrate you and know that your special gift can and will change someone's life. It's not only possible, it is downright probable.

Chapter 9

Don't Be Buried Alive

"I can do all things through Christ who strengthens me."

—**Philippians 4:13**

Y ou know what the scariest place on earth is?

The scariest place on earth is the graveyard. Not because of spirits and ghosts, but because of all the wasted dreams and potential that are buried deep beneath the earth....all the unfulfilled, decaying dreams and goals that were buried alive and not shared with the world.

Has anyone ever asked you this question: Where do you see yourself a year from now? Five years? Ten years from now?

If you have no goals set in place to nurture that gift (your greatness), they will be buried with you in the graveyard.

What would your tombstone read? Here lie Jane's dreams. She had great ideas; she would have served so many people well if she would have taken the time to pursue that fire that was burning in her soul.

We cannot go back in time and finish the unfinished when we are dead. The time is now. There are no tomorrows, there are only todays, and that is only a moment at a time. We are not promised anything.

Are you willing to take the risk that tomorrow is going to be here for you or are you going to act at this moment in time, the moment that you have right in front of you right now and start living your true purpose?

Take the time to dream, but remember that dreams need action to develop. Don't go to the grave with all that greatness still inside of you. Ask yourself every day if you are making good use of this treasured gift called time, which once lost, is gone forever.

I want my tombstone to read:

"Here lies Pat, who lived a life of passion every day. She unwrapped her gifts and brought joy and love to the world. Each day was exciting, fun and productive. Pat lived a meaningful life, and she lived her dreams. She died happy."

This, my friend, is what I want for you. A life that is meaningful and fulfilled.

This book was written as a reminder and guide for you to open those unlocked doors of potential and greatness that has been and always will be inside of you. Open each one up with love, and nurture them every minute like a newborn baby. Don't let that evil twin take hold of you. You are way better and much stronger than that. Our evil twin whispers vicious lies that we are not enough, and those words get stuck in our subconscious mind until we hear them over and over again. Break through that barrier and set yourself free. To overcome that evil twin, stop nurturing it because it is not serving you.

Life can throw a lot of choices at you and you sometimes forget your direction. It can get so overwhelming that you may start listening to what other people are telling you to do instead of doing what you want to do. You become someone else's ideal. You lose your identity. Where did you go wrong, you ask? In reality, you are not lost; you just got swept up in other people's opinions and values. Stay true to yourself and know deep in your heart what you need to do in this world -- and get out and do it!

You can have an amazing life using your gifts and talents. Don't let fear rob you of your joy and stunt your development. Be the person that God intended you to be. Don't let the last words out of your mouth be "I should have....." You only get one life and only YOU have the choice to live it the way you want to. No one is stopping you but you. You can face the challenges that your choices bring, and use your faith and determination to overcome them. Give it all you've got, stand up tall, and leave a legacy.

"The meaning of life is to find your gift. The purpose of life is to give it away."

—Pat Pilla

I hope with all my heart that what I wrote in this book resonated with you and that you now feel you can take on the world with a different and more positive attitude, approach, and mindset. My mission is for you to see your full potential and utilize the unique gifts with which you were born.

I want you to see that you are filled with love and that you are here to make the world a better place, one heart at a time. I want you to see that you can let go of who you think you were supposed to be and embrace who you really are.

There is only one YOU, a uniquely and wonderfully made creature of God. You have been given authority and dominion over all things. You *CAN* do *ALL* things. Don't let anyone else value you more than you value yourself. Remember perception equals progression. However you perceive yourself is how others will perceive you. Hold yourself to a higher standard. Do not limit yourself.

"When God breathed His life into you, He placed a blessing on you the overrides anything that's trying to hold you back. The blessing God has for you cannot be stopped by bad breaks, by people, or by injustice. God is not limited by our circumstances."

—Unknown

Stay hungry! Stretch your mind with new tasks. Always learn and grow. Knowledge is the key to success. We can never know too much. Train yourself to be uncomfortable being comfortable. Associate with successful people and see what makes them tick. Observe how they are different from non-achievers.

Pray and constantly feed your subconscious with positive feedback.

Develop a sense of urgency. Take action – it doesn't have to be perfect. Just do it and don't waste time overthinking and getting yourself into an analysis paralysis Do something NOW that will move you towards your goal. Ask yourself, what are you waiting for? Do what you can do today instead of waiting until tomorrow.

Take responsibility for your life and stop blaming others for your past failures. It is up to you to accomplish your dream. No one else is going to do it for you. Repeat affirmations like "I am worthy," "I am capable," "I am valuable," "I can do all things," "I am loved."

Act as if you are already there. Yes! Roll play! The more you act out who and what you want to be, the more you will believe it. The more you believe it, the faster you will become what you wish. As it is said, we all want what we don't have. The desires of your heart are special.

Whether it is fame, fortune or love, the reason you desire it is because those things are hard to get. They take work. It's not like a peanut butter and jelly sandwich that you can whip up in your kitchen; it takes determination and a fire in your soul. It won't happen overnight.

Though the desires of our heart may be difficult to achieve, the secret is to act as if it has already happened to you. I know it sounds cliché, but the more you act as if you're already there, the more you start believing you can achieve it and the more motivated you become to reach that desire. It's all about mindset. We can't obtain *everything* we desire, but I do believe we obtain what we need. You attract what you put out.

Look … it is not easy to just start acting like the person you want to be; it helps to seek out people who are already where you want to be and learn from them. Build yourself a strong foundation based on love, trust, faith, and knowledge that will withstand the test of time. Step into the role you were made for and always serve with a grateful heart.

Please let me know if my book resonated with you, and you are ready to share your gift with the world.

I would love to connect with you. ***All you have to do is e-mail me here:*** nocrapcoach@gmail.com

Look forward to hearing from you.

I will leave you with one last quote.

"It does not matter whether we have been given great talents, abilities and wealth, or very little. What matters is whether we make good use of what we have been given, whether large or small."

—Unknown

May God bless you on your special journey and always.

Much Love,

Pat

ACKNOWLEDGMENTS

I f I were to acknowledge ALL the people that I love and admire and who made me into the woman I am today, there would not be a big enough book to hold all the names. You know who you are and I cannot express my love and gratitude to you.

You have been with me since day one and have not left my side. Your prayers have helped me move mountains. You have truly impacted me on my journey of transformation and I would never be where I am today without you.

I praise and thank God every single day that He put you in my path to support and guide me. I am truly blessed and totally overwhelmed by all of your love and the support you gave me when I thought I couldn't go on

Thank you, and may the Lord continue to bless each and every one of you. The love you have shown me is now being paid forward. My cup is overfilled.

SPECIAL THANK YOU

I want to dedicate a special thank you to Maria Piazza. She gave up her most precious time to work on the editing of this book. I could not have done this without your expertise and your unconditional love and support. I am truly blessed by you Maria and touched by your awesomeness. Thank you from the bottom of my heart.

A special thank you to AJ Mihrzad, who not only wrote the foreword for my book, but without him there would be no book. AJ, you have been my striving force, not only in my weight loss journey but you also inspired me to take action and to tell my story. I have pushed through many obstacles in my life because of you and I am forever grateful. You will always have a special place in my heart. "DTJD"

Here is a huge shout out to Christine Dupre. I cannot thank you enough for designing my book cover. You hit the nail on the head with this one, and it is just perfect. To be able to see my vision was totally awesome—you are one talented human being. Thank you for being part of this awesome adventure. I am truly grateful for you and may you continue to reap all of God's blessings.

ABOUT THE AUTHOR

Pat Pilla was born in Brooklyn, New York. She had a major turning point in her life when she said, "Enough is enough!" with her health and weight issues. Through her struggles, and ultimately peeling off layers upon layers of self-inflicted garbage, she was able to change her mindset and lost over 200 pound. With a lot of prayer and believing that God said everything is possible through Him, she forged ahead and never looked back.

As she started to recognize her unique gifts, she opened up an online baking business, selling portion-controlled cheesecake bonbons that landed her on TV, on *Macy's Million Dollar Makeover.*

Soon after, she realized that her true passion was to help people find their unique gifts, strengths, and purpose in this world. Now Pat coaches people from all over the world to be the best version of themselves, to remove their self-doubt and believe that they have a special place in this world to serve others and pay it forward.

Pat also speaks at seminars and shares her genuine love of all people no matter where they are in life or how old they are. She brings hope to the lost through her faith in God and shares her wisdom of what she had gone through so that people know you can always change the life you have to the one you desire by one simple word: "Choice."

Pat now lives in New Hyde Park, New York with Mike, her husband of forty years. She has a daughter, Jennifer, and a son-in-law, Loren, and loves spending time with two most spectacular and precious grandsons, Elijah and Noah. She loves to have fun and see with the innocent eyes of a child.

Pat loves to travel and meet people from all walks of

life. You will find her in the warmer months riding around in her dream convertible when she's not off inspiring everyone to be their best selves!

Her mission is to show people how to love who they are and reveal to them how they are uniquely and wonderfully made. Each person brings something special to the table and is a gift to the world.

Pat will continue on her journey to help others until her last breath is taken here on Earth. Her passion and determination is endless.

"We create our tomorrows by what we dream about today"

—Pat Pilla

Made in the USA
Columbia, SC
15 December 2017